ORGAN DONATION

RISKS, REWARDS, AND RESEARCH

Corona Brezina

ROSEN
PUBLISHING®

New York

Published in 2010 by The Rosen Publishing Group, Inc.
29 East 21st Street, New York, NY 10010

Library of Congress Cataloging-in-Publication Data

Brezina, Corona.
Organ donation: risks, rewards, and research / Corona Brezina. — 1st ed.
    p. cm. — (In the news)
Includes bibliographical references and index.
ISBN-13: 978-1-4358-5275-4 (library binding)
ISBN-13: 978-1-4358-5556-4 (pbk)
ISBN-13: 978-1-4358-5557-1 (6 pack)
1. Donation of organs, tissues, etc. — Juvenile literature. I. Title.
RD129.5.B74 2010
617.9'5 — dc22

                                                              2008044646

Manufactured in the United States of America

On the cover: Clockwise from upper left: A doctor washes a liver prior to transplantation; heart-kidney transplant survivor Ardell Lien and his wife address the press after he sailed solo around the world; doctors perform a live-donor kidney transplant.

contents

How Organ Donation Works

1

Organ donation.
The gift of life

Orga
The g

The concept behind organ donation is simple: remove a healthy organ of the body, such as a heart or kidney, from a donor; transplant that organ into a recipient, a patient whose organ is failing. The operation will give the recipient a second chance at leading a healthy life.

Turning this concept into reality was one of the great medical breakthroughs of the twentieth century. Fifty years ago, the failure of a major organ led to the patient's death. Today, organ transplantation is routine, with a high rate of success.

From the time of the first experiments, organ transplantation and organ donation have caused controversy. Those who did not believe that organ transplants were possible criticized the earliest pioneers in this field of medicine. Today, about 15,000 organ transplants are performed each year in the United States alone. But these are not the stories that tend to make headlines. Most news stories concerning organ transplantation and organ donation instead focus on controversial issues, unusual cases, and medical breakthroughs.

Media, such as newspapers, magazines, television news, and the Internet, also play a role. Many find organ donation to be an uncomfortable subject. They do not like thinking about surgeons cutting up bodies to remove organs. Therefore, people can be strongly affected by occasional news stories about irresponsible or criminal incidents related to organ donation. Such stories can negatively influence people's viewpoints about the entire system.

One recent high-profile case involved a laboratory called Biomedical Tissue Services. In 2005, the New Jersey–based company was shut down for illegally selling body parts stolen from corpses. The criminals took tissues and bones from bodies without the knowledge or permission of family members. They also forged legal documents, often lying about the age and cause of death. As a result, hundreds of patients received tissue and bone grafts from unknown donors with unknown medical histories.

The Biomedical Tissue Services scandal caused shock and pain for innocent patients. Indirectly, such scandals that cause people to distrust the concept of organ donation could also affect patients in need of organ transplants. Today, organs for transplants are in such huge demand that there is a shortage. There are far

An X-ray reveals that workers for Biomedical Tissue Services stole bones from a body and replaced them with plumbing pipe.

more people waiting for lifesaving organs than there are organ donors. In a sense, this present-day situation is a result of the overall successes in the field of organ transplantation, which was once considered a far-fetched experiment.

Early History of Organ Donation and Transplantation

Physicians explored the idea of transplantation as early as the European Renaissance (c.1300s–1600s). During that era, they found that they could take tissues from one part of a person's body and graft them—surgically attach them—to a damaged site. They also found, however, that transplants between two people did not work. Nevertheless, doctors and scientists continued experiments with animals, making important medical advances as they went along. About the year 1900, doctors discovered that there were three major blood groups: A, B, and O. For a successful blood transfusion, or transfer between two individuals, the donor's blood type must match the recipient's type. In 1906, an eye doctor performed the first successful transplant of a cornea—the transparent layer covering the eye. Corneal transplants are easier than organ transplants because they do not require connecting veins or other vessels.

Many of the first attempts at organ transplantation focused on the kidneys. These organs filter waste out of the blood and produce urine. Humans have two kidneys, but it is possible to live with only one functional kidney. Early experiments included human-to-human transplants, as well as transplants involving kidneys from animals.

The first successful kidney transplant was performed by surgeon Joseph E. Murray, in 1954. He removed one kidney from twenty-three-year-old Ronald Herrick and transplanted it into Ronald's identical twin brother, Richard, who was experiencing kidney failure. The organ began functioning immediately. Richard lived a healthy

Ronald Herrick (*left*) poses with Dr. Joseph E. Murray in 2004, fifty years after Murray performed the first successful kidney transplant.

life for nine more years before dying of a heart attack. In cases that did not involve identical twins, though, the patient's body rejected the transplant. Gradually, researchers began to understand that the recipient's immune system was involved in organ rejection.

The immune system is the body's means of defending itself against disease. It protects the body from bacteria, viruses, and other foreign invaders. It recognizes cells that do not belong and responds by attacking and destroying them. Organs transplanted from identical twin donors worked. However, in order to perform transplants between unrelated donors, doctors would have to learn how to prevent an immune response.

One experimental method involved treating patients with full-body radiation (X-rays) before the transplant operation. This process suppressed the immune system, but it was risky and produced unreliable results.

Researchers then began to develop special drugs, called immunosuppressants, in order to prevent rejection.

In 1963, American physician Thomas Starzl performed the first liver transplant, followed by four more. Unfortunately, every one of the recipients died within days of the operation. Starzl returned to the lab, focusing on animal experimentation. He discovered that a combination of immunosuppressive drugs greatly improved the chances for survival. In 1967, Starzl performed the first successful human liver transplant. Due to advances in immunosuppressive drugs, doctors soon performed

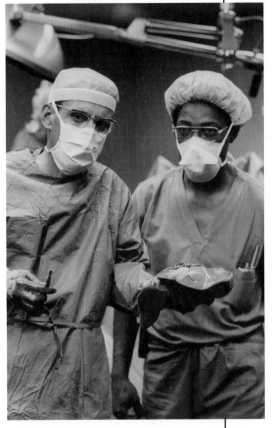

Surgeon and researcher Dr. Thomas Starzl (*left, holding liver*) performed groundbreaking work in transplantation.

the first successful transplants of the heart, pancreas, and lungs. (The pancreas is an organ that plays a role in digestion.)

As rates of success increased, ethical concerns about transplantation became more pressing. Medical ethics involves standards of honorable conduct for doctors. The field of bioethics addresses concerns about what is right and what is wrong when it comes to medical and scientific research. The issue of ethics had arisen in the very first kidney transplant. In order to donate a kidney to his twin brother, Ronald Herrick had to undergo a risky surgery. A basic guiding principle for doctors is, "Do no harm." Did removing a kidney from a healthy man violate medical ethics? Today, transplants from living donors are widely practiced and accepted. Still, new issues have emerged about the ethics of donating and receiving organs.

Advances in Organ Donation Since the 1980s

Better immunosuppressive drugs improved survival rates and reduced negative side effects for transplant patients. More and more transplant centers opened in the United States and across the world. The field of transplantation became increasingly standardized and regulated. In 1984, the U.S. Congress passed the National Organ Transplant Act (NOTA). The act called for a task force to study the issues surrounding organ donation and transplants. It also banned the sale of organs for transplantation in the United States.

The task force recommended uniform standards for the various steps of the donation and transplant process. NOTA led to the creation of the Organ Procurement and

Transplantation Network (OPTN), which connects the various groups involved in an organ transplant. In 1986, a nonprofit organization called United Network for Organ Sharing (UNOS) was organized to run OPTN. Since then, the U.S. Congress has passed several measures aimed at encouraging organ donation. In 2004, for example, the Organ Donation and Recovery Improvement Act (ODRIA) was signed into law. The act made funds available for organ donation and made it easier for donors to consider live organ donation.

Researchers in transplantation continue to make new breakthroughs. In 1998, doctors performed the first hand transplant. In 2005, French surgeons performed the first partial face transplant on Isabelle Dinoire, whose face had been mauled by a dog. Doctors transplanted a nose, mouth, and chin from a deceased donor. The procedure was a success, but hand and face transplants raise further ethical concerns. Unlike patients in need of a heart or kidney, the recipients of face or hand transplants are not in danger of death if they do not undergo the operation. Afterward, they will probably need to take immunosuppressive drugs for the rest of their lives to avoid rejection of the transplant. These drugs can involve serious risks and side effects. The debate continues as to whether or not these extreme measures should be taken in cases when the patient's life is not at stake.

Carrying an organ donation card can eliminate any doubt or confusion over a person's wishes in case of crisis.

Organ Donation Today: By the Numbers

The National Organ Transplant Act of 1984 led to the creation of the Scientific Registry of Transplant Recipients (SRTR). This database keeps track of every aspect of organ donation and transplants.

According to SRTR data, there were 8,024 deceased donors whose organs were recovered for transplants in 2006. ("Deceased donor" is the term for an organ donor whose organs are collected after death.) Out of these, 1,642 had died as a result of automobile accidents, the most common circumstance of death. A total of 28,311 organs were recovered from these donors, including hearts, lungs, kidneys, pancreases, livers, and intestines. Living donors, on the other hand, donated 6,730 organs for transplants.

The most frequent organ transplant during 2006 was the kidney, with 16,646 transplants performed. Next was the liver, with 6,136 transplants performed, then the heart, with 2,147 transplants, and the lungs, with 1,401 transplants.

Success is measured by how long the recipient survives following the transplant. Among recipients from deceased donors, the survival rate after three months was about 98 percent for kidney recipients, 93 percent for liver recipients, 92 percent for heart recipients, and 93 percent for lung recipients. After three years, the survival rate was about 88 percent for kidney recipients, 79 percent for liver recipients, 80 percent for heart recipients, and 68 percent for lung recipients. After ten years, the survival rate was about 61 percent for kidney recipients, 60 percent for liver recipients, 54 percent for heart recipients, and 27 percent for lung recipients.

At the end of 2006, there were 93,820 people on waiting lists for organs. The organ most in demand was the kidney, with 66,961 people needing the organ. Out of the total number on the lists, 41,776 fell in the 50–64 age range. About 58 percent were male, and 42 percent were female. Of these, 15.5 percent had already received one organ transplant.

Between 1997 and 2006, the waiting list grew from 53,375 people to 93,820. By the end of 2008, the number exceeded 100,000. During the period between 1997 and 2006, the number of transplants performed only grew from 20,093 to 28,291. Every year, thousands of patients die waiting for an organ.

The Importance of Organ Donors

In 2007, James Burdick offered testimony before a U.S. House of Representatives subcommittee on the importance of strengthening organ donor programs. Burdick was the director of the Division of Transplantation within the U.S. Department of Health and Human Services. He outlined the facts about transplantation in the United States and pointed out that, every day, nineteen people die waiting for an organ.

Considering the shortage of organs for transplants, it is critical that people register as organ donors. In some states, driver's licenses indicate whether or not someone has registered as an organ donor. In others, registered donors carry organ donor cards. If a registered donor dies, then his or her organs will be recovered for donation to transplant recipients. Registered organ donors should inform their families of their decision to become a donor, as it often falls to families to make the final decision.

Nevertheless, many people do not take the step of registering as an organ donor. Often, this is because they do not imagine that they might meet their end anytime soon. Sometimes, though, people simply don't understand organ donation and, therefore, are unwilling to register as a donor. Some wrong ideas about organ donation are not credible, yet they persist. For example, a popular Internet chain e-mail describes a situation in which a person wakes up in pain after being drugged and kidnapped. A nearby note explains that his kidneys have been removed to be sold on the black market. Another much-repeated rumor tells of a network through which babies from Latin America are transported to the United States for their organs to be harvested for transplants. In truth, there is no illegal trafficking of human organs in the United States.

People may be unsure about whether their religion approves of organ donation. In fact, most religions permit organ donation and transplantation, though some have special rules. For Jehovah's Witnesses, for example, organs must be drained of blood before being transplanted. Muslim religious leaders, once opposed to

Organ shortage is a problem worldwide. These are applications for British citizens who want to register as organ donors.

organ donation, have reversed their stance. Some Buddhist funeral practices involve long rituals, often too lengthy for the organs to remain usable.

Some people may think that they are too old for their organs to be useful. They may believe that because of medical conditions, they are not allowed to donate. This may be the case, but they should still register as donors. Medical professionals will judge whether or not one's organs or tissues are usable for donation.

Organ donation does not have negative consequences for the donor or for the donor's family. Being a registered organ donor does not affect treatment in case of an accident or other medical condition. The first priority for the hospital staff is to save the patient's life. The individual's status as an organ donor is relevant only after death has occurred. The donor's family does not have to pay for any costs related to organ donation. Organ recovery is performed surgically, so it does not cause damage that would affect funeral arrangements.

Organ allocation is the process of deciding which patients will receive organs. Some people may not want to donate because they believe that the organ allocation system is unfair. Because there is a shortage of organs for transplants, some of the policies and guidelines behind organ allocation are controversial. Nevertheless, a patient's place on the transplant waiting lists for organs is based on medical considerations. A patient's wealth or celebrity status does not give him or her an advantage. It is true, though, that patients generally must have insurance coverage or other means of paying in order to be approved for a transplant.

The Organ Transplant Process

In 1995, baseball legend Mickey Mantle had a failing liver. His condition was caused by decades of alcohol abuse. Doctors found that Mantle also had a tumor in his liver, which they believed might be cancerous. In addition, he was infected with the hepatitis C virus, probably acquired during a blood transfusion earlier in his life.

Mantle's doctors added his name to the United Network for Organ Sharing (UNOS) liver waiting list. Without a transplant, he could be expected to survive only two or three weeks. Less than two days after Mantle was put on the waiting list, a donor liver became available. Doctors performed the transplant, and Mantle's new liver began functioning. Five weeks after the transplant, a scan showed that Mantle's cancer had spread to his lungs. Despite aggressive medical treatment, he died less than two months later.

As soon as the hospital had announced that there was a donor liver for Mantle, there was public outrage.

Former baseball star Mickey Mantle waves during his first news conference after receiving a new liver.

Almost nobody believed that Mantle would have received the organ so quickly if he had not been a celebrity. Some said that Mantle's doctors had made the wrong decision in agreeing to a liver transplant in a patient who had cancer. Others criticized the system for allowing a transplant for an alcoholic who had recklessly destroyed his own liver. They claimed that there were candidates for the transplant who were more deserving of a liver.

After the furor died down, most observers concluded that Mantle had not received special treatment. He had reached the top of the regional waiting list due to medical considerations, not celebrity status. At the time of the allocation, there were no signs that his cancer had spread. The organ allocation system will not give organs to current alcoholics or drug abusers, but it does not take lifestyle history into account. Nevertheless, the incident demonstrates the importance of setting fair organ allocation policies. For people on waiting lists, small policy changes could mean the difference between life and death.

Candidacy for Transplants

A patient's transplant journey begins with a diagnosis of end-stage organ failure. This means that there is no treatment other than a transplant that can save his or her life. Next, the patient's doctor may refer him or her to a transplant center—a hospital or other medical center that operates transplant programs. There are 252 transplant centers in the United States. Not all provide transplants of every major organ. There are a total of 243 kidney transplant programs, for example, and 130 heart transplant programs.

Next, the patient meets with a transplant team. A transplant coordinator, usually a nurse, manages the patient's care. There is a transplant surgeon and a transplant physician, who is a nephrologist (kidney doctor), cardiologist (heart doctor), or other specialist. A dietitian works with the patient before the transplant and during recovery. Other team members include a financial coordinator, an insurance case manager, and a social worker. In addition, transplant patients receive care from nurses, technicians, physical therapists, psychiatrists (doctors who specialize in mental health), and pharmacists.

The transplant team begins by figuring out whether or not the patient is a candidate for a transplant. This will involve extensive interviews and tests. Not every patient qualifies as a candidate. Transplant candidates must be sick enough that a transplant is their only option but not so sick that there is an uncertain likelihood of survival. In addition to medical factors, the team considers financial and psychosocial issues. Psychosocial factors include family conditions, mental health, and patient history.

Heart, lung, and liver transplant candidates will die without a donor organ. Many kidney patients, however, can choose whether or not a transplant is the best option. Some with kidney failure can survive through a medical procedure called renal dialysis. This generally requires the patient to visit a hospital several times a week for sessions on a dialysis machine, which performs some of the kidney's functions.

Carol Playfair (*left*) was given a new chance at life after her sister Tracey (*right*) volunteered to donate a kidney.

Some transplant candidates do not have to wait for a donor to become available. They may have a family member or a friend who is willing to become a living donor. Less frequently, they may receive a "directed donation" through the wishes of a deceased donor's family. Otherwise, the candidate will be added to the UNOS organ waiting list so that he or she can be matched to a donor.

Organ Allocation

UNOS coordinates organ procurement (collection) and allocation among various member organizations. These include transplant centers, organ procurement organizations (OPOs), and histocompability labs. OPOs, sometimes called organ banks, arrange for donation with the deceased donor's family. They also evaluate whether or not donation is medically suitable. If so, they then recover the organs and arrange for transportation. Usually, the OPO checks for a local match. When there is no local match, UNOS matches the organ to a candidate in the national database. Histocompatibility labs test donors and possible organ recipients to check if the tissues are a good match. Like blood types, there are several different tissue types. Matches in tissue type between donor and recipient are not essential. However, recipients with a good match often have a higher survival rate.

When an organ becomes available for a transplant, the UNOS computer generates a list of matches. Several factors determine possible matches. The donor and recipient must have the same blood type. For some transplants, such as kidney transplants, tissue type is also important. For some organs, such as the heart, size matters. A heart donated from a small woman, for example, would not be able to pump blood for a tall man with a large frame. For some organs, such as the liver, medical urgency is considered. A candidate with the most serious need for the organ will be given priority over a candidate with a lesser need. In addition to medical factors, distance between the donor and recipient may be taken into account.

UNOS specialists then contact the transplant team of the first match on the list. The team has one hour to decide on whether or not to accept the organ. If the patient is not ready for an immediate transplant, or if the patient is not healthy enough to handle a major operation at that time, then the team will decline. UNOS continues to offer the organ to the next matches on the list until it is placed.

Oversight of the allocation system is not perfect. There have been instances in which transplant programs have cheated in order to receive an organ. For example, in 2003, three Chicago hospitals were accused of lying about patients' medical status in order to move them up on the waiting list. One patient, listed as critically ill, was dining out at a restaurant when he was notified that there was a donor organ for him. In 2003, a California medical center improperly accepted a donor liver for a Saudi patient. This misallocation skipped over dozens of patients on the waiting list.

Finding a donor match is a matter of critical importance for any candidate, but certain individuals may have even greater cause for concern. Members of some racial and ethnic groups, for instance, may have higher rates of certain diseases that can lead to organ failure. Native Americans have an extremely high rate of diabetes, which can cause failure of the kidneys and pancreas. African Americans and Hispanics have high rates of kidney disease. Often, the best donor match for a transplant candidate is a member of the same racial or

Actor and comedian George Lopez received a donor kidney from his wife, Ann, in 2005.

ethnic group. The candidate is less likely to experience rejection of a donor organ when it is a good match. High rates of disease among members of these groups lead to an even greater need for donor organs.

A Second Chance

An organ transplant is a complicated and lengthy operation. A kidney transplant takes about three hours. A liver transplant may last for ten hours or even longer if things don't go smoothly. The procedures for receiving the organ and performing the operation vary depending on whether or not the donor is living or deceased. (See chapters 3 and 4.) On rare occasions, a patient in need of a lung transplant may receive a heart and lung "bloc" from a deceased donor. This is done when doctors believe that the donor lungs will work better with the donor heart. If the lung recipient's heart is healthy, then it can be donated to a patient in need of a heart transplant.

After the surgery, the patient wakes up in the intensive care unit. He or she may be connected to a breathing tube. Various other tubes inserted into the patient's veins deliver antibiotics (medicines that prevent and treat infections), painkillers, and other fluids. There will be drains around the incision where the organ was inserted. Medical professionals will closely monitor the patient's condition and judge when he or she is ready to be discharged from the hospital.

During recovery, the patient begins adjusting to life with a transplant. A transplant offers a second chance at life, but a transplant recipient must make lifestyle changes. For some people, living with a transplant is like living with a persistent medical condition. The recipient must regularly take numerous drugs and visit the hospital for tests and checkups. Every minor medical issue seems like a potential crisis, especially immediately following the transplant.

Organ Rejection and Immunosuppressant Drugs

The transplant recipient's worst fear is rejection of the organ. When rejection occurs, the body's immune system tries to destroy the organ. The worst, and rarest, type of rejection is hyperacute rejection. Doctors observe hyper-acute rejection immediately, during the operation. The second type, acute rejection, usually occurs less than a month after surgery. In most cases, acute rejection can

If this two-year-old patient is lucky, his partial liver transplant will function so well that he may be able to stop taking immunosuppressive drugs.

be reversed by aggressive treatment with antirejection drugs. The third type is chronic rejection, in which the organ gradually deteriorates and ceases to function well.

Rejection is combated by a combination of immuno-suppressive drugs. Because immunosuppressants weaken the immune system, transplant recipients are at a high risk of infection. This can make recovery difficult, for a minor infection can have serious health consequences. The immunosuppressants must work well enough to prevent rejection. However, the dosage should be as low as possible so that the patient will not be left too vulnerable to infection. As the patient recovers, his or her doctors refine the types and doses of medications.

In the long term, organ transplant recipients have a higher-than-average risk of developing cancer, a result of immunosuppression. In some cases, cancer treatment may require the patient to stop taking immunosuppressive drugs. This puts the patient at risk of losing the transplanted organ.

3 Living Donors

Every year, thousands of transplant candidates receive organs from living donors. The kidney is the most frequently donated organ, with 6,436 transplants of kidneys from living donors performed in 2006. However, living donors can give several other organs, too. A living donor can give a segment of his or her liver, since the donor's liver grows back afterward. In 2006, there were 287 living donor liver transplants in the United States. It is also possible, though not common, for living donors to donate part of a lung, a portion of the pancreas, or a portion of the intestine. These organs do not grow back, but it is possible for the donor to live a healthy life with a partial organ.

Giving Life

A transplant candidate is very fortunate if he or she receives an organ from a living donor. The recipient will not have to be added to the organ waiting list. Also, the operation can be scheduled ahead of time. There is no chance of the transplant team declining an organ because the candidate has a cold. The organ does not have to be transported from one hospital to another. And recipients of living donor organs have a slightly higher survival rate than recipients of deceased donor organs.

Most living donors are close family members or friends of the recipient. Non-related donors typically include spouses, in-laws, neighbors, coworkers, or other friends.

Non-directed donors are donors who do not know the recipient. They donate their organ out of a desire to help another person. They are also called anonymous donors, altruistic donors, and stranger-to-stranger living donors. These types of donors are quite uncommon.

Sometimes, a transplant candidate has a willing living donor, but they do not share the same blood type. This problem may be resolved through a paired donation. Say, for example, that recipient A and recipient B both have donors who wish to donate a kidney, but neither candidate shares a blood type with their donor. Transplant coordinators can arrange for recipient A to receive an organ from recipient B's donor, and vice versa. Both transplant operations are performed at the same time.

In 2008, surgeons at the Johns Hopkins Hospital in Maryland performed a six-way kidney swap. Their

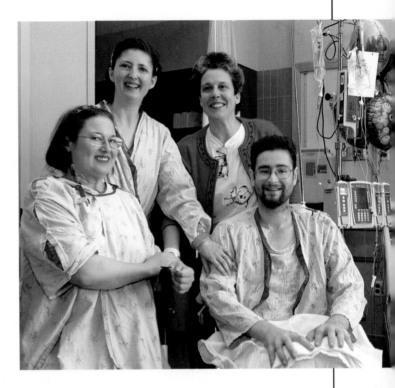

Paula Lipinski and Doug Lillibridge (*front row*) received kidneys through a paired donation with Claudia Lillibridge and Celia Lipinski (*rear*).

computer software identified five patients who all had potential living donors with the wrong blood or tissue type. When a non-directed donor was added to the formula, it worked out that every patient could receive a match. The last kidney was allocated to a candidate on the UNOS kidney waiting list. The twelve operations lasted ten hours and involved nine transplant teams, six operating rooms, and about one hundred medical personnel.

Qualifying to Be a Living Donor

Transplant recipients owe their health—and often their lives—to the organ donor. The transplant system, and society as a whole, also benefits when a living donor gives an organ. Every single organ donor expands the pool of donor organs available for transplant candidates. But living donors realize that there are risks.

In 2002, fifty-seven-year-old Mike Hurewitz volunteered to donate part of his liver to his brother, fifty-four-year-old Adam Hurewitz. Liver transplants are the most difficult organ transplants. The liver is a very large organ, so doctors must make a wide incision, or cut, across the belly, just underneath the rib cage. There are four major blood vessels connected to the liver, and many of the first liver transplants failed because the patient began bleeding uncontrollably during surgery. Today, donors generally receive the right lobe, or section, of a living donor's liver. This is about two-thirds of the organ. Surgeons estimate that the death rate for a living donor is 0.5 to 1 percent.

Adam Hurewitz recovered after receiving part of his brother's liver in a transplant performed at Mount Sinai Hospital in New York City. Mike Hurewitz, the donor, choked on his own blood in the recovery ward and died three days after the surgery.

The case revived ethical issues about living donor transplants. People debated if it was right or wrong for doctors to perform an operation that had the potential to cause a healthy person's death. Living donors say they believe that saving the organ recipient's life is worth the low health risks. Others disagree.

Because of the risks, potential living donors are thoroughly screened before doctors approve the donation. Living donors must be healthy and in good shape physically. Medical conditions like diabetes, high blood pressure, cancer, and heart disease disqualify a person from becoming a living donor. Donors are also tested to be sure that they are a match for the recipient. Race and sex are not factors in donating an organ.

The donor must also sign an informed consent form. This process ensures that he or she understands every phase of living donation, including the risks. It

Transplant surgeon Hootan Roozrokh, seen here at his arraignment in 2007, allegedly hastened the death of a disabled man in order to collect his organs. In 2008, a jury found him not guilty.

is important that living donors do not feel forced in any way into donating an organ. Professionals inform the donor of alternative treatments for the recipient, such as deceased donation. They also alert him or her to any of the recipient's existing medical conditions, such as diabetes or age-related factors, which could lead to serious consequences after the transplant.

Organ donation is major surgery. Medical risks include death; organ failure (which could require transplant); infection; and unforeseen, long-term complications. The patient may feel pain and fatigue afterward. In addition, the donor may experience psychological consequences. Any surgery requires a recovery time, during which the patient may feel anxious or depressed. For organ donors in particular, news of medical setbacks for the transplant recipient can be emotionally devastating.

Potential donors are made aware of the financial issues involved in organ donation as well. The recipient's insurance covers the medical costs of donation. Nevertheless, the donor may have to take time off of work. Programs sometimes reimburse travel, lodging, and other expenses, but this is not guaranteed. Medical complications, such as high blood pressure in a living kidney donor, may affect future health insurance costs.

Transplant programs require donors to return for follow-up visits for two years after the donation. This is so that the programs can collect information on the long-term health consequences for donors. Follow-up reports are entered into national databases.

A Living Donor Kidney Transplant

The choice to become a living donor is not final. At any stage, the donor can decide not to donate. For a living donor kidney transplant, the donor and recipient both check into the hospital a day or two before surgery. Both patients are made unconscious using general anesthesia. Then, the two surgeries are performed at the same time, since doctors prefer the organ to be outside of the body for only a short period.

The surgical removal of a kidney is called a nephrectomy. The kidneys are not perfectly symmetrical. The transplant surgeon often chooses to remove the left kidney whenever possible, since the left kidney has a longer renal vein. This makes it more convenient to transplant. Also, the right kidney is more difficult to remove because it is positioned behind a rib.

There are two types of nephrectomy: open and laparoscopic. In both procedures, the kidney is removed after cutting blood vessels and the ureter (the tube that carries urine). The surgeon flushes the kidney with a preservation solution and passes it to the recipient's transplant team. The recipient's transplant surgeon makes an incision, puts the kidney in place, and connects the vessels and ureter. The recipient's own kidneys are generally not removed because the extra step of removing them is usually unnecessary and may increase recovery time. The transplant takes three to four hours.

Often, the recipient recovers more quickly than the donor. This is because in an open nephrectomy, muscles

A surgeon handles a donated kidney during transplant surgery.

are cut to remove the kidney. Implanting the kidney in the donor does not require cutting as much muscle. For laparoscopic nephrectomy patients, recovery time is shorter, since the incisions are not as extensive.

Donors usually stay in the hospital for four to seven days. Full recovery takes four to eight weeks. A donor who has had an open nephrectomy is left with a long, curving scar running from below the rib cage toward the back. A donor who undergoes laparoscopic nephrectomy is left with several smaller scars around the navel.

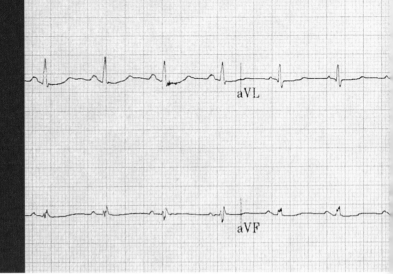

4 Deceased Donors

Most donor organs are recovered from deceased donors. When a person dies, oxygen no longer circulates through the blood, and the body's organs quickly start to deteriorate. In order to be usable for transplant, an organ must be recovered quickly after death. After one hour, organs will lose function.

Generally, doctors do not wait for the heart to stop beating. Most organs are recovered from patients who have been declared brain dead. Brain death is different from ordinary death. It is also different from a coma, which is a potentially reversible state of unconsciousness. There are very specific medical and legal guidelines for declaring a person brain dead. According to the Uniform Determination of Death Act (UDODA) of 1981, "An individual who has sustained either (1) irreversible cessation of circulatory and respiratory functions, or, (2) irreversible cessation of all functions of the entire brain, including the brainstem, is dead." In other words, a person is brain dead when the brain no longer

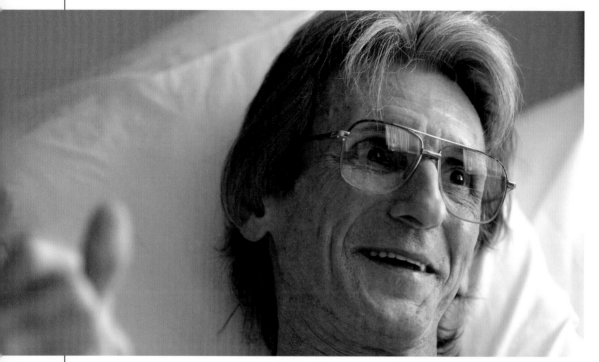

Steve Skaggs (*above*) recovers from a lung transplant. His deceased donor was able to give seven organs to five different people.

receives blood or oxygen, or else when there is no activity in the brain.

There is no doubt about brain death, as various tests are performed to confirm that there is no brain function. If it is possible that lack of responsiveness is due to drugs or alcohol, doctors wait eight hours before declaration of death. There has never been a case in which a person recovered after brain death. Two doctors must independently determine that the person is brain dead.

A brain dead donor can be kept alive on a ventilator, which is a machine that keeps a person breathing. He or she may also need fluids and other medical care to stabilize the body's physical condition.

Donation After Cardiac Death

In the 1990s, due to the organ shortage, doctors began transplanting organs from expanded donors. "Expanded donors" is a term that refers to a larger pool of potential organ donors that in the past were not considered suitable for transplant. Examples include the elderly or people with certain medical conditions. If a transplant candidate will die without a new organ, then transplantation of a less-than-optimal donor organ may be the better option. Doctors will not perform a transplant if they do not believe the operation will be a success.

Expanded donors also include non-heartbeating donors. These are deceased donors who died when their hearts stopped, rather than through a declaration of brain death. Called donation after cardiac death (DCD), it often occurs at a hospital after a patient's doctor and family decide to remove him or her from life support. After death is pronounced, five minutes must pass. If the patient does not take a breath or show a heartbeat, then the organ recovery team can begin retrieving the organs.

In 2008, three organ retrievals from infants sparked controversy about DCD. In one instance, transplant surgeons began retrieving organs three minutes after the cardiac death of the infant. In the other two cases, surgeons waited just seventy-five seconds. Reducing the wait time increases the chances that the donor heart can successfully be transplanted. This is good news for infants in need of a heart transplant, as one in four dies before receiving a donor organ. Still, the practice raises ethical issues. Cardiac death is defined by irreversible loss of function. If the heart can function after the transplant, then it means the loss of function was not truly irreversible.

Procuring an Organ

The recovery of a donor organ is a massive process. According to Frank Stuart's *Organ Transplantation*, it can involve from twenty to one hundred people and can cost as much as $25,000. The process begins with representatives from the organ procurement organization (OPO) approaching the potential donor's family. These individuals are trained to discuss the matter in a sensitive and tactful manner. Once consent is given, the OPO

(*Opposite page*) A surgeon removes a donor kidney from its outer plastic bag in preparation for a transplant operation.

coordinates the next steps, which include learning about the donor's medical history, running lab tests, recovering the organs, and finally, transporting the organs.

Often, several teams attend an organ procurement, each recovering a different organ. The removal sequence is heart and lungs, liver and pancreas, intestines, kidneys, and then cornea, bone, and tissues like skin, heart valves, and tendons. After the organs are recovered, they are preserved for transportation. Generally, they are flushed with a solution that will protect them from damage. The team packs each organ in a triple layer of plastic bags, places it in a rigid container, and puts it in a cooler full of ice. Next, they make arrangements for the organs to be transported—by land or sometimes air—to transplant centers. Time is critical. A kidney can be preserved for as long as thirty hours, but hearts and livers must be transplanted within four to six hours.

Meanwhile, other professionals gather the details of the donor's medical history. They ask about circumstances of death, medical conditions, medications, previous surgeries, and any drug and alcohol use. Certain conditions, such as the diseases HIV and hepatitis, rule out donation. (HIV is the virus that causes AIDS; hepatitis is a viral infection that affects the liver.) Each organ is thoroughly examined and tested.

In 2007, four organ donor recipients in Chicago contracted HIV and hepatitis C after their transplants.

They had all received organs from the same donor. The transplant centers had followed the correct procedures before the transplants, but the results of the HIV test were incorrect. According to the U.S. Centers for Disease Control and Prevention (CDC), this was the first time in twenty years that HIV had been transmitted by an organ donor.

The Heart Transplant

A heart transplant candidate's wait ends when a donor organ becomes available. If the patient is not already hospitalized, then he or she must immediately report to the transplant center. It is vitally important that the donor heart remains out of the body for only a brief time. Often, the transplant team starts getting the patient ready for the transplant before the donor heart is delivered.

Once the organ has been approved, the patient is anesthetized and put on a heart-lung bypass machine. In this process, the blood vessels from the heart are severed and connected to tubes leading to the machine. This will circulate and add oxygen to the blood during the operation. The machine also cools the patient's body temperature to about 86° Fahrenheit (30° Celsius) to prevent damage to the other organs.

In most cases, the surgeon then removes the patient's heart. Next, the surgeon begins the delicate task of attaching the patient's blood vessels to the donor heart. The heart often starts pumping as soon as the vessels are connected. When the transplant team is sure that the heart is working, the patient is gradually taken off of the heart-lung bypass machine and is sewn up. A heart transplant operation usually lasts about five hours or less.

The patient is closely monitored after the transplant. If there are no complications, then he or she can usually check out of the hospital after about a week. Transplant recipients are required to return for frequent checkups for the first few months after the operation. The primary concerns are rejection and infection.

In 2003, seventeen-year-old Jésica Santillán received a donated heart and set of lungs at Duke University Hospital in North Carolina. Santillán had suffered from a deformed heart. The transplant failed, however, because of an error at the hospital. Santillán had type O blood, but her donor

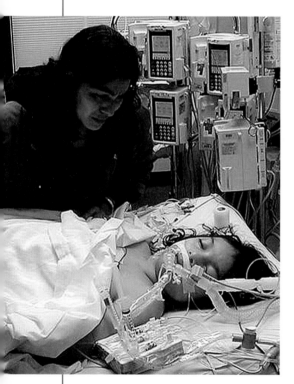

Jésica Santillán's mother, Magdalena, visits her daughter in the hospital after the unsuccessful transplant operation.

heart was type A. Her body immediately began to reject the organs. She received a second transplant days later, but there were complications following the surgery. Doctors declared her brain dead and removed her from life support.

Santillán's case is a tragic exception. Most heart transplants result in success, made possible through the extraordinary generosity of organ donors and their families. Because organ donor families are so important, OPOs make sure that they are given follow-up information on the success of organ recovery and transplant if they wish to know. Organ recipients often express their gratitude in a letter to their donor's family, although OPOs do not reveal donors' identities.

5
Issues Surrounding Organ Donation

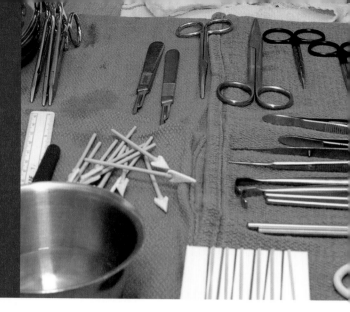

I n 2003, a forty-eight-year-old Brooklyn woman faced death unless she received a kidney transplant. She had been on a transplant waiting list for seven years without receiving a donor organ. The woman, who did not give her name to the *New York Times* for a story on the subject, turned to the black market.

She contacted Ilan Peri, an "organ broker" in Israel. After negotiations, her kidney transplant was performed in South Africa. Her donor was thirty-one-year-old Alberty da Silva, a poor Brazilian who saw the sale of one of his kidneys as a chance to make a fortune. According to authorities, Peri's organ-smuggling ring provided pass-ports and air tickets for both the recipient and the donor. The woman paid more than $60,000. Da Silva received $6,000, although he was robbed of most of the money during his return trip to Brazil.

Investigators from Israel, South Africa, and Brazil broke up the smuggling ring. This one case, however, did not go far in shutting down the black market for human

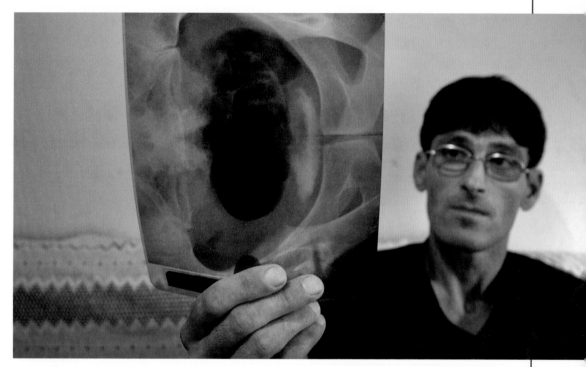

A Bosnian man holds an X-ray of his kidney. He is willing to sell the organ illegally to get the money he needs to rebuild his war-torn home.

organs. Although it is illegal in most countries to sell human organs, this does not stop shady organ brokers or donors who badly need money. The illegal organ trade is known to operate in India, Pakistan, China, the Philippines, and other countries. Donors in these countries have died after the removal of their kidneys. In addition, they are often cheated out of their promised payment.

As long as there is a shortage of donor organs for transplants, there will be a market for illegally sold organs. One of the most pressing issues in organ donation and transplants is how to increase the supply of organs.

Possible solutions include changes in government policy and breakthroughs in scientific research.

Examining Policies of Organ Donation and Transplants

There have been many efforts made to educate the public and increase organ donation. Since 1983, the third week of April has been National Organ and Tissue Donation Awareness Week. The Gift of Life Congressional Medal Act, which recognizes organ donors and their families, was passed in 2001. In 2003, April was declared National Donate Life Month. Behind the scenes, transplant programs, hospitals, and OPOs work to improve the coordination of organ recovery.

Rates of organ donation have increased slightly but not enough to match demand. Some observers have called for bolder policy changes. One possibility is enacting presumed consent for organ donation in the United States. Instead of filling out donor registration cards if they do wish to donate (as they do now), people would fill out opt-out cards if they do not wish to donate. Those who support presumed consent say that it would greatly increase the number of organs available for transplants. Another approach is mandated choice, which would require people applying for a driver's license to specify whether or not they want to donate, do not want to donate, or are undecided.

The most controversial proposal is to allow for the sale of human organs. The more extreme plan calls for organs to be bought and sold just like any other type of goods. Living donors or the families of deceased donors would be paid prices depending on supply and demand of organs. The milder "incentive approach" would compensate donors and their families but would not give them direct payment. Possible compensation includes lower taxes, payment of funeral expenses, health insurance,

Seventy-one-year-old Ardell Lien, a heart-kidney transplant recipient, sailed around the world in order to raise organ donation awareness.

or coverage of medical expenses. Those in favor claim that financial incentives are worth considering because they would increase the number of donors and save thousands of lives every year.

One of the major objections to payment for donation is that any such system would take advantage of the poor. The poor would feel pressured to donate, whereas the rich would feel no pressure at all. Another objection is that organ donors should donate because they want to save lives, not make money. Also, many believe that using the human body to make a profit is below human dignity.

Organ allocation is still a problem, too, raising many practical and ethical questions. Who should get an organ? Should it be the person who is sicker and, therefore, has a more urgent need? Or, should it be the person who has the best chance of a positive outcome? A young recipient would get more years of life from an organ than an older recipient, so should age be considered? Should an alcoholic with liver disease be rewarded with a donor liver ahead of a non-alcoholic whose disease was not a result of poor lifestyle choices? Should prisoners receive transplant organs? These are all valid questions. In the end, however, policymakers tend to focus on medical considerations in allocating organs. Trying to allocate organs to the more "deserving" candidate would imply that one person's life is more valuable than another's.

The Future of Organ Donation and Transplants

The entire debate over organ donation and transplants could change if scientific advances create new treatment options. Many areas of research, though promising, seem unlikely to yield practical results anytime soon. Still, just a century ago, most people considered organ transplantation unrealistic.

Some scientists are pursuing research that could make it easier for transplant recipients to lead normal, healthy lives. They are looking for ways that patients could live without immunosuppressants. These drugs can have unpleasant side effects and cause long-term health problems. A small segment of liver recipients, however, can stop taking immunosuppresants without experiencing rejection. This is known as spontaneous liver transplant tolerance. If scientists could learn how to bring about tolerance in other transplant patients, then it would be a great breakthrough.

Stem cell research could open new possibilities for transplant candidates. Stem cells can develop into any type of cell or tissue. Someday, perhaps, stem cells introduced into a damaged organ could repair it directly. Stem cell research is controversial, though, because the most useful stem cells come from human embryos, which are destroyed in the process.

What if, instead of transplanting an organ from a human donor, the organ came from another source? Many see promise in artificial organs, or implantable machines that could perform the function of a heart, lung, or other organ. In 2001, fifty-three-year-old Robert Tools became the first person implanted with an artificial

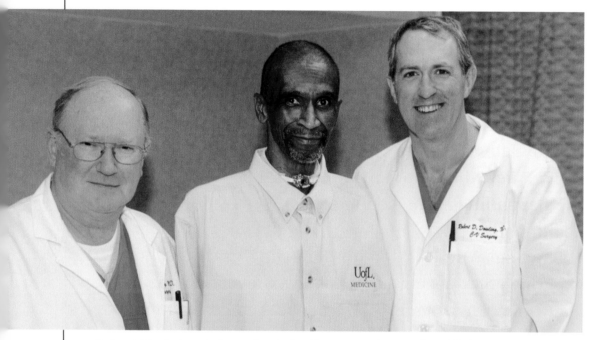

Robert Tools (*center*) received the first experimental artificial heart after he was diagnosed with end-stage heart failure.

heart. The device extended his life for nearly five months. Today, most artificial organs are "bridges" that can help an organ function until a donor organ is obtained.

Some also see promise in bioartificial organs. These would be organs made of living cells but created in the laboratory. This type of work involves cell and organ engineering. Researchers have already been able to successfully engineer bioartificial versions of skin. Sometime in the future, perhaps, a candidate in need of a new organ may simply supply a doctor with a sample of his or her own cells. The organ would then be grown in a laboratory.

Animals are a third alternate source of transplantable organs. This type of transplantation is called xeno-transplantation. Researchers have already performed experiments in transplanting animal organs into human recipients. The most famous case occurred in 1984. "Baby Fae" was born three weeks premature with a heart defect. When she was one week old, she had to be put on life support. It was very doubtful that a donor heart would become available, and a pediatric cardiac surgeon—a doctor specializing in children's heart surgery—suggested an experimental treatment. Baby Fae's parents agreed to the transplant of a baboon heart. The transplanted heart started beating during surgery, and Baby Fae began breathing without the help of a respirator. Unfortunately, eighteen days after the surgery, her body began rejecting the organ. She died shortly afterward.

Researchers still cannot prevent rejection of xeno-transplants in most cases, though there has been great progress in the field of xenotransplantation since 1984. One promising area of research is in pigs, which have organs similar to human organs. In experiments, pigs have been genetically altered so that humans would be less likely to reject their organs. Someday, a transplant candidate checking into the hospital to receive a new xenotransplant organ may see an organ donor pig in the operating room next door.

Glossary

allocation Process of distributing organs based on a system of policies and guidelines.

anesthetize To make insensitive to pain.

brain death State in which cerebral and brain stem function have ceased irreversibly.

candidate Person in need of a transplant whose name is on an organ transplant waiting list.

cardiac Pertaining to the heart.

cessation Stoppage, as of the heartbeat or other bodily functions.

controversy Dispute, often public, between sides holding opposing opinions.

dialysis Medical procedure that performs some kidney functions, including removal of some waste products from the blood.

donor Individual who gives organ(s) or tissue for transplantation.

end-stage Late, fully developed phase in the course of a disease.

ethics Rules or standards governing the conduct of an individual or the members of a profession.

graft To surgically remove a body part, such as tissue, and reattach it to another part of the body or to another individual. Also, a graft is the term for a transplanted organ or tissue.

immune system Body's system that protects against foreign invaders, such as viruses and bacteria.

immunosuppressant Medication that prevents rejection of a transplant organ by reducing immune system functioning.

incision Cut made during surgery.

procurement Removal of organs from a donor for transplantation.

rejection Process in which the immune system recognizes a transplanted organ as foreign and attacks it.

renal Pertaining to the kidneys.

stem cell Unspecialized cell found in fetuses, embryos, and some adult body tissues that has the potential to develop into all types of specialized cells.

tissue Collection of cells in the body, such as blood or bones, that carry out a specific function.

ventilator Machine that assists breathing in cases of respiratory failure.

xenotransplantation Transplantation of organs between members of different species.

For More Information

Canadian Association of Transplantation
10207-107 Street
Fort Saskatchewan, AB T8L 2H9
Canada
Web site: http://www.transplant.ca
This Canadian national nonprofit association is committed to facilitating and enhancing the transplant process.

Organ Donation and Transplant Association of Canada
55 Eglinton Avenue E., Suite 312
Toronto, ON M4P 1G8
Canada
(866) 949-0003
Web site: http://www.organdonations.ca
This nonprofit organization is dedicated to encouraging Canadians to become organ donors and supporting related medical research.

TransWeb
3868 Taubman Center
1500 E. Medical Center Drive, SPC 5391
Ann Arbor, MI 48109
(734) 764-4141

Web site: http://transweb.org
TransWeb is a comprehensive resource of donation and
transplant information.

United Network for Organ Sharing (UNOS)
700 North 4th Street
Richmond, VA 23219
(804) 782-4800
Web site: http://www.unos.org
This not-for-profit organization administers the Organ
Procurement and Transplantation Network (OPTN).

Web Sites

Due to the changing nature of Internet links, Rosen
Publishing has developed an online list of Web sites
related to the subject of this book. This site is updated
regularly. Please use this link to access the list:

http://www.rosenlinks.com/itn/orgd

For Further Reading

Ballard, Carol. *Organ Transplants*. Milwaukee, WI: World Almanac Library, 2007.

Egendorf, Laura K., ed. *Medical Ethics*. Farmington Hills, MI: Greenhaven Press, 2005.

Fullick, Ann. *Rebuilding the Body: Organ Transplantation*. Chicago, IL: Heinemann Library, 2002.

Green, Reg. *The Gift That Heals: Stories of Hope, Renewal, and Transformation Through Organ and Tissue Donation*. Bloomington, IN: AuthorHouse, 2008.

MacLachlan, Patricia. *Edward's Eyes*. New York, NY: Atheneum, 2007.

McClellan, Marilyn. *Organ and Tissue Transplants: Medical Miracles and Challenges*. Berkeley Heights, NJ: Enslow Publishers, Inc., 2003.

Miller, G. Wayne. *The Xeno Chronicles: Two Years on the Frontier of Medicine Inside Harvard's Transplant Research Lab*. New York, NY: PublicAffairs, 2005.

Schwartz, Tina P. *Organ Transplants: A Survival Guide for the Entire Family*. Lanham, MD: Scarecrow Press, Inc., 2005.

Starzl, Thomas E. *The Puzzle People: Memoirs of a Transplant Surgeon*. Pittsburgh, PA: University of Pittsburgh Press, 1992.

Bibliography

Archibold, Randal C. "Girl in Transplant Mix-Up Dies After Two Weeks." *New York Times*, February 23, 2003. Retrieved October 1, 2008 (http://query.nytimes.com/gst/fullpage.html?res=9C07E2D7113DF930A15751C0A9659C8B63&sec=&spon=&pagewanted=1).

Ellingwood, Ken. "A Second Chance at Life for Gravely Ill Teenager." *Los Angeles Times*, February 21, 2003. Retrieved October 1, 2008 (http://articles.latimes.com/2003/feb/21/nation/na-transplant21).

Finn, Robert. *Organ Transplants: Making the Most of Your Gift of Life*. Sebastopol, CA: O'Reilly, 2000.

Goodwin, Michele. *Black Markets: The Supply and Demand of Body Parts*. New York, NY: Cambridge University Press, 2006.

Gordon, Serena. "Infant Heart Transplant Controversy Continues." *U.S. News and World Report*, August 13, 2008. Retrieved October 1, 2008 (http://health.usnews.com/articles/health/healthday/2008/08/13/infant-heart-transplant-controversy-continues.html).

Grady, Denise. "Donor's Death at Hospital Halts Some Liver Surgeries." *New York Times*, January 15, 2002. Retrieved October 1, 2008 (http://query.nytimes.com/gst/fullpage.html?sec=health&res=9400E2D91338F935A25752C0A9649C8B63).

Healthcare Systems Bureau. "Testimony Before Committee on Oversight and Government Reform, Subcommittee on Information Policy." Census and National Archives, U.S. House of Representatives, September 25, 2007. Retrieved October 1, 2008 (http://www.hhs.gov/asl/testify/2007/09/t20070925a.html).

Health Resources and Services Administration. "2007 OPTN/SRTR Annual Report: Transplant Data 1997–2006." Retrieved November 1, 2008 (http://www.ustransplant.org/annual_reports/current/).

Johns Hopkins Medicine. "Hopkins Performs Historic 'Six-Way-Domino' Kidney Transplant." Media Relations and Public Affairs, April 8, 2008. Retrieved October 1, 2008 (http://www.hopkinsmedicine.org/Press_releases/2008/04_08_08.html).

Munson, Ronald. *Raising the Dead: Organ Transplants, Ethics, and Society*. New York, NY: Oxford University Press, 2002.

Murphy, Timothy F. "Gaming the Transplant System." *American Journal of Bioethics*, Vol. 4, No. 1, January 2004, p. 28. Retrieved October 1, 2008 (http://www.bioethics.net/journal/pdf/4_1_IF_w28_Murphy.pdf).

Parr, Elizabeth, Ph.D., and Janet Mize, R.N. *Coping with an Organ Transplant: A Practical Guide to Understanding, Preparing for, and Living with an Organ Transplant*. New York, NY: Avery, 2001.

Petechuk, David. *Organ Transplantation*. Westport, CT: Greenwood Press, 2006.

Powell, Michael, and David Segal. "In New York, a Grisly Traffic in Body Parts." *Washington Post*, January 28, 2006. Retrieved October 1, 2008 (http://www.washingtonpost.com/wp-dyn/content/article/2006/01/27/AR2006012701569.html).

Rohter, Larry. "The Organ Trade: A Global Black Market; Tracking the Sale of a Kidney on a Path of Poverty and Hope." *New York Times*, May 23, 2004. Retrieved October 1, 2008 (http://query.nytimes.com/gst/fullpage.html?res=9C0CE0DD163EF930A15756C0A9629C8B63&sec=health).

Steenhuysen, Julie. "Four Chicago Transplant Recipients Contract HIV." *New York Times*, November 13, 2007. Retrieved October 1, 2008 (http://www.nytimes.com/2007/11/13/health/13cnd-organ.html?ref=health).

Stuart, Frank P., et al. *Organ Transplantation*, 2nd ed. Georgetown, TX: Landes Bioscience, 2003.

Tilney, Nicholas L. *Transplant: From Myth to Reality*. New Haven, CT: Yale University Press, 2003.

Zarembo, Alan, and Charles Ornstein. "Deception Behind Liver-Transplant Switch Proved to Be Fatal." *Los Angeles Times*, October 13, 2005. Retrieved October 1, 2008 (http://articles.latimes.com/2005/oct/13/local/me-liver13).

Index

ethical issues of, 9–10, 11,
32–33, 40
financial issues of, 17, 34
future of, 50–53
medical risks of, 34
recent advances in, 10–11
and religion, 15–16
statistics on, 12–14
Organ Donation and Recovery
Improvement Act (ODRIA), 11
organ procurement, 22, 40–43
organ procurement organizations
(OPOs), 22–23, 40–42, 45, 48
Organ Procurement and
Transplantation Network
(OPTN), 10–11
organ rejection, 25, 27–28, 51

P

presumed consent, 48

R

renal dialysis, 21

S

Santillán, Jésica, 44–45
Scientific Registry of Transplant
Recipients (SRTR), 12
spontaneous liver transplant tolerance, 51
Starzl, Thomas, 9
stem cell research, 51

T

Tools, Robert, 51–52
transplant team, members of,
20–21

U

Uniform Determination of Death
Act (UDODA), 37
United Network for Organ Sharing
(UNOS), 11, 18, 22, 23, 24, 31

X

xenotransplantation, 53

About the Author

Corona Brezina has written more than a dozen titles for Rosen Publishing. Several of her previous books have explored topics related to science and current events, including *In the News: Climate Change* and *Careers in Forensics: Medical Examiner*. She lives in Chicago.

Photo Credits

Designer: Tom Forget; Editor: Christopher Roberts
Photo Researcher: Cindy Reiman